Vincent de Paul

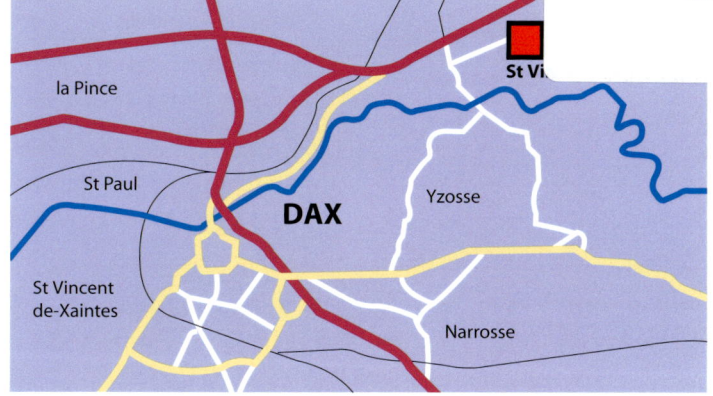

Out of the marshes

"de Paul" may sound a bit posh, but it probably just means "from the marshes".

Vincent's family would have taken its name from the marshlands that surrounded their farmstead in the South-West of France, not all that far from Lourdes. The express train from Paris should have you there in under four hours. The nearest village was called *Pouy*, though it has since changed its name to *Vincent de Paul* in honour of its most famous citizen. The original Baptismal font is still in use in the village church, where in 1581 the seeds of faith in Jesus Christ were first sown in Vincent.

A road-sign points the traveller to *Le Berceau* – "the cradle" – a mile or two from the village. Here Vincent was born. The old family home still stands. Also standing nearby, with a bit of support, is an 800 year old oak tree. It has survived a lot, including

an attempt by a few crazed revolutionaries to burn it down in the 1790s. Under it, surely, Vincent the boy would have sheltered from the hot suns and Atlantic storms, so typical of this region of Gascony.

Nowadays this area is heavily forested, but in Vincent's youth it would have been an open, marshy land of rough pasture. The young Vincent would have stalked the marshes on stilts as he moved through his flocks of sheep, cattle and swine. As well as keeping his feet dry, this way of getting around would have helped him to keep a look-out for danger. Perhaps it also gave him a sense of distant horizons.

Family

Six children were born to Jean de Paul and his wife Bertrande de Moras. First came four boys: Jean, Bernard, Vincent, and Dominic; and then two girls, both christened Marie, but known as Mengine and Claudine. Vincent seems to have been the brightest and most alert of them. And his father saw possibilities in having him educated. Here was an investment from which all the family might eventually benefit. So in 1594 the de Pauls tightened their belts and sent Vincent off to *Dax*, where the Franciscans had a school.

The Berceau: the house where Vincent grew up in, is on the far-left of the picture.

Schooling

In later life, Vincent modestly used to refer to himself as "a scholar of the Fourth Form" – perhaps to discourage his Community from having notions about themselves. In fact he was to receive a lot of education, spending seven or eight years at university, mostly in *Toulouse*, and probably teaching theology there for a short time. Later he took a Degree in Canon Law in Paris – which proved to be very useful in regard to the various religious foundations he was involved with.

Values learned and never forgotten

Vincent never lost a sense of the values of the country peasants among whom he had grown up. The more he saw of city life, and the goings-on among the rich and influential, the more his admiration grew for those who tilled the soil and shepherded flocks.

He was a man who believed in the value of hard work : his priests were to earn their bread by the strength of their

arms and the sweat of their brows, as the peasants did. Nor was there a trace of sentimentality in this: Vincent was too much of a realist for that. His experiences convinced him that the hard-working peasants were particularly blessed, and part of him always regretted that circumstances had taken him from that way of life. But such are the providential ways of God, that in due time he was drawn back to these country people through the parish missions given by himself and his priests.

A priest at twenty

During the time he was studying in Toulouse, Vincent put himself forward for ordination to priesthood, and was ordained by the Bishop of *Perigeux*. He was nineteen or twenty years of age, though mature and focused : already,

for example, he had established his own school to help pay his university fees.

Gradually his understanding of priesthood became more and more elevated, and in later life we find him saying :

"as for myself, had I known what it was when I had the temerity to enter it – as I have come to know since then – I would have preferred to till the soil than to commit myself to such an exacting state of life. I have said this more than a hundred times to poor country people when, to encourage them to live contentedly as upright persons, I told them I considered them fortunate in their situation……the older I get, the more convinced I am of this…"

Perhaps it was to mark his ordination, that he made his way down to Rome in early 1601– the first of two visits. He tells us that he was moved to tears by the experience, not least by the saintliness of the then Pope, Clement VIII.

Vincent in Slavery

After finishing his studies in Toulouse in 1604, Vincent's life took a really odd turn – an interlude of a few years in which it has proved impossible to separate fact from fiction. Two letters turned up towards the end of his life – letters written by himself fifty years earlier – with an extraordinary story.

The letters say that in order to collect some money that was owing to him, he had ridden a long way on horseback to Marseilles; but that then, on taking ship from there to Narbonne, to shorten his journey home, he was captured by Turkish pirates, and ended up in the slave market in Tunis, North Africa.

Firstly, he was sold to a fisherman; then to an alchemist who was absorbed in trying to turn base metals into gold: Vincent proved to be a dab hand at managing the numerous furnaces necessary for this enterprise. He also learned from his master how to operate a "talking skull", and became an adept ventriloquist.

Then he was sold on to an apostate Christian who had three wives, one of whom was attracted by Vincent's character and obvious spirituality; for in these difficult circumstances he had remained true to his priestly vocation. She used to get him to sing the Psalms to her, and was so impressed that she persuaded her husband to return to his Christian faith.

Eventually all four of them escaped across the Mediterranean back to France.

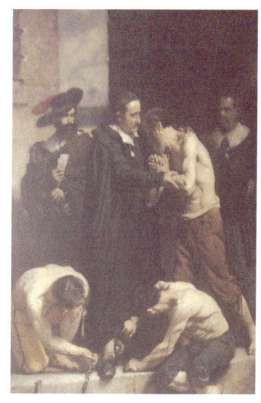

Losing his Faith ?

Take the Paris metro to *Marie de Clichy* in the western suburbs of the city, and you will find yourself near the church where, in 1612, Vincent had his first parish. Though he would speak of it as one of the happiest periods in his life, it coincided with a time of severe trial. He had met a theologian whose spirit was in turmoil because of great temptations against his faith. Vincent was so moved by his distress that, in prayer to the Lord, he offered to undertake these doubts himself in place of this tortured soul.

And that is what happened. The theologian had his peace of mind restored, but now Vincent was overwhelmed with doubts about the faith. His way of coping with these was to place a copy of the *Creed* in a pocket near his heart, and touch it at moments of exceptional stress. This cloud was to hang over him for about four years, and only lifted after he promised God that he would dedicate the rest of his life to serving the poor.

Vincent's old church, Clichy-la-Garonne

The experience was crucial in Vincent's spiritual journey. Ever afterwards he could face any poor person, for he had been brought to realise that he himself was the poorest of the poor, absolutely in need of God's sustaining mercy. And on his deliverance, he knew that he was the richest of men, because he now believed in a real, personal way that he was loved by the Lord.

Parish Missions

I stand in a village church in Picardy in Northern France, and gaze at the pulpit. Here, on a freezing January day in 1617, Vincent de Paul, a long way from home, had a deep insight into what God wanted him to do with the rest of his life.

The village is called *Folleville*, which some say translates as "the town of the foolish ones". The local people insist that the name derives from a nearby wood; the French word being much the same as the English word foliage. It was one of hundreds of villages owned by the de Gondi family, who had vast estates in northern France.

At the insistence of Mme. de Gondi, his employer, Vincent

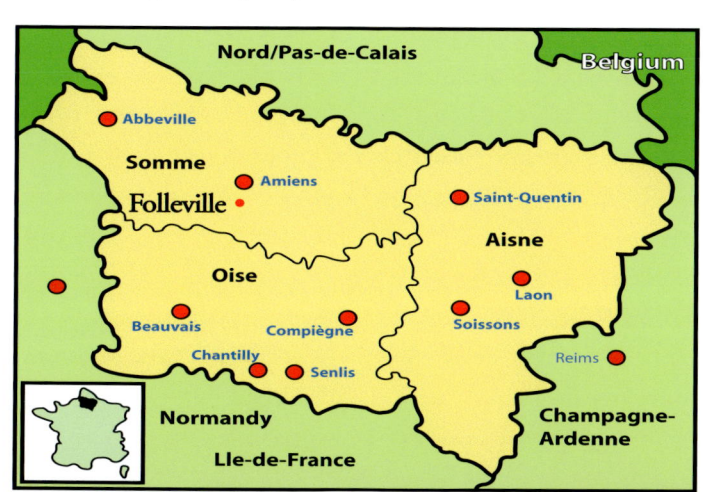

The old pulpit in Folleville

was preaching to the illiterate peasants of *Folleville* - the sort of people he would have grown up among - when he was taken hold by the very words with which Jesus Christ proclaimed his own mission : *"the Spirit of the Lord has anointed me ; and has sent me to bring Good News to the poor."*

Mysteriously, Vincent realised that this was what he himself was now being called to do. These poor people, in their need, were crying out to him for the saving word of God; and he sensed that they, and their like, would somehow be at the centre of his life for the rest of his days. It was a moment of special revelation. Already, he was in his thirty-sixth year, so you might say that it had taken quite a while for him to reach this simple point of clarity about his future. But during that time, the peasant soil of his heart had been thoroughly harrowed and nurtured. Now it was ready to receive the seed of a special mission.

The immediate occasion of his moving sermon, had been a pastoral call to the bedside of a dying man. This man had a reputation in the locality for being a good person, but his conscience was not at peace, for he had been concealing serious sins for much of his life. Now he made a general confession of all his past sins to Vincent, and experienced such relief and joy that he called his family and neighbours to his sick bed, and told them all about it. Vincent realised that there must be thousands of country people like this penitent, burdened with spiritual anxieties, and dying without the sacrament of reconciliation. The realisation disturbed him greatly, and when facing the congregation at *Folleville* became convinced that something should, and could, be done about it.

The Vincentians

Gradually Vincent came to understand that what was required was that a group of missioners should give themselves completely to the work of preaching and teaching among the rural communities of France; for by and large no one else was doing this work. The poor country people were marginalised, spiritually as well as economically; but fortunately the de Gondis had become concerned about the spiritual fate of their tenants. So they offered to support the sort of group of evangelising priests, that Vincent had in mind, in order that missions could be given free of charge.

And so it happened that a community of priests known as the **Congregation of the Mission** (*Vincentians*) came into being. Vincent liked to refer to them as "The Little Company" – a reference to the low-profile calling he saw for it. And in keeping with this ideal, their style of giving missions to the country people was to be simplicity itself, especially in their manner of preaching and

The pulpit in the old Church in Clichy that Vincent would have used.

catechising. This was essential, if people were to grasp the core doctrines of the Christian faith.

It became the custom to have catechism sessions for the children and elderly around midday, and for working adults in the evening, when their day's labour in the fields and in the home was over.

The people were encouraged to make a general confession of their sins and receive Holy Communion. In fact, that was the aim of the parish mission : a true, personal conversion, for both people and pastor. And, indeed, it was the missioners' practice to remain in the parish until everyone had made a general confession.

The Cry of the Poor

"when that the poor have cried, Caesar hath wept" (Shakespeare).

Vincent, too, may have wept, but he also decided to do something about it.

In the year 1617, he spent a number of months as Pastor in a country town in Burgundy, called *Chatillion* – not far from the village of *Ars*, whose saintly Curé, John Vianney, would make his mark a few centuries later. This was an important posting for Vincent, for it gave rise to the first **Confraternity of Charity** – a sort of fore-runner of the St. Vincent de Paul Society – which would minister to the sick, the poor, and the lonely.

What happened was this : Vincent was vesting for Mass one day when word was brought to him that there was a destitute family a few miles out of town, who needed urgent assistance. He appealed from the pulpit on their behalf, and did so with such eloquence that half the congregation were soon on their way with help of various kinds.

Vincent saw that people were only too willing to share with those in need, but that this good-will, to be effective, had to be regulated. And, crucially, he proved to have a supreme talent for organisation and tactful leadership in such matters.

Thus, the Confraternities were born. They not only saw to the distribution of food and clothing among the needy, and the visiting of the lonely, but also arranged for the sick to be attended to with true kindness.

As things turned out, the two most significant aspects of the Confraternities were, firstly, the systematic way in which they went about their business; and secondly, the involvement of lay people in leadership roles.

The Confraternities spread, all over France – initially wherever a parish mission was conducted; but then further

One of Sr. Catherine Labouré's visions of Our Blessed Lady in the Rue du Bac

afield as their usefulness became obvious. The men's, and mixed Confraternities, did not do so well, but those made up exclusively of women, flourished. Women, for the first time in history we might say, were suddenly given public leadership roles to an extent that was unheard of in either church or secular society.

They became known as **Ladies of Charity**. From the nature of the case they tended to be women of a certain social class and education. And they found in Vincent an inspired animator. Quite a number of them had been widowed at a young age – their husbands killed in duels or warfare. Vincent brought purpose to their devastated and often empty lives. Such was his personality, and the spiritual authority which he radiated, that he seemed to effortlessly make friends with people, whatever their background. He won the trust of many of the nobility, and was continually coaxing and cajoling them into sharing their wealth with the poor – often with great success. And some of them became outstanding leaders in the Confraternities.

Vincent's favourite women

Gradually it was realised that the "hands-on" work of ministering to the wretched, could best be done by women, of strong character, who were closer in class to those among whom they would work. It has been said that Vincent had in mind peasant girls like his own sisters – girls used to the hard life of the countryside, and not afraid of getting their hands dirtied.

The community of young women who gradually

formed around this ideal, had an inspirational leader in *Louise de Marillac*. At first Vincent was her spiritual director. Gradually they became colleagues and friends, as together they tackled the social problems that racked France. And jointly they undertook the guidance of the many women who would be their assistants in bringing the love and compassion of Jesus Christ to those who most needed it. These women came to be known as **Daughters of Charity** – Vincent's admiration for them was boundless : he used to refer to them as Daughters of God.

Their institution was a radical departure - absolutely without precedent. Never before in the western world – nor the eastern world, for that matter - were women to move freely, and unprotected through society's most dangerous dark recesses as angels of mercy, empowered only by the love of God. And, of course, it was unheard of – illegal in fact - for a Religious sisterhood to be so liberated – with the slums as their "cloisters" : this was tearing up the Rule-book. It was truly audacious. A stroke of genius.

Never before had the sick been looked after in their own homes like this by visiting nurses. And all work for the poor and infirm was done free of charge.

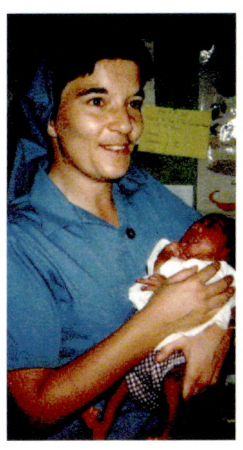

Wherever there was a human need, the Daughters were to be found. And the needs were endless. France seemed to be continually at war, with the usual consequences for the ordinary people: homelessness, contagion and starvation. And there were always those whom government didn't want to know about: the orphaned and widowed; convicts and galley-slaves; the mentally ill, disturbed adolescents, abandoned infants. All were to be treated by the

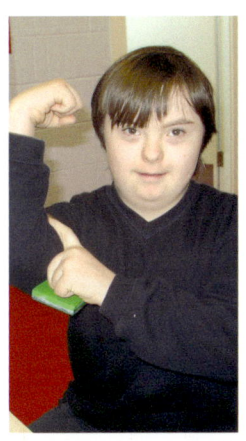

Daughters with the greatest respect. Vincent encouraged them to open schools for poor girls wherever they went.

Physical danger was at its height for the Sisters among the convicts and galley slaves. Here were desperate, vicious men; angry and embittered. Men without hope.

The Daughters bought food for the prisoners and prepared their meals. They washed their clothes, looked after those who were sick, scrubbed their cells, repaired their mattresses, made new garments for them - became in effect their servants. And all the while they had to run the gauntlet of mockery, insults, insolence and lewd suggestions. The Daughters tried to disarm the prisoners through their gentleness and compassion, knowing that they had been deeply wounded by a merciless system.

Vincent was always encouraging: *"Nothing is more meritorious in God's eyes than charitable work for poor prisoners;"* and typically he led from the front, frequently moving among these hapless wretches, and trying to give them some hope, and a sense

Blessed Mary Magdalene Fontaine and three other D.C.'s, who were guillotined in Cambrai, 1794.

of their own worth in the eyes of God.

A work with which the Daughters became especially associated was the care of abandoned infants – many of them born to near-destitute, single women. These eventually were getting such priority when it came to funding, that some of the missioners grumbled that, as a result, the parish missions were becoming under-financed and neglected.

Vincent was saddened to hear the complaints – he thought they were at variance with the spirit of the Gospel. This concern for abandoned children was a great advance – the Daughters were to treat them with special affection – they were to be taught to read and write; taught skills and given every chance to take their place in society.

Remarkably soon, the Sisters' distinctive butterfly bonnets were to become one of the most welcome and immediately recognisable images in all of France. Disgracefully, several of these servants of the poor were guillotined during the irrational frenzy of the French Revolution.

Delivered from Jansenism

By one of those odd quirks of history, Vincent when he was a young priest, found himself

Vincent de Paul. Chapel of the Rue du Bac.

lodging with a man who was to become the leading proponent of Jansenism in the 1600s. His name was *Jean Duvergier*. They became friendly – recognising in one another a high idealism for the things of God.

But Duvergier's spirituality became increasingly narrow and gloomy – a sort of Catholic Calvinism – with an unbalanced emphasis on a wrathful God. Vincent had already been blessed by winning the friendship of the great *Francis de Sales*, Bishop of Geneva, whose dealings with the Calvinists there were a by-word for charity, and wisdom. Vincent learned moderation from Francis, and the value of gentleness in dealing with souls. He learned the primacy of God's love and mercy for all; and speaking of this became a feature of the Vincentian parish missions.

Letters and talks:

As well as giving thousands of spiritual talks – to the clergy, the Daughters, the Ladies of Charity, to country people on the missions, the galley slaves, and so on, Vincent also found time to keep in touch with innumerable people by letter.

There may have been as many as twenty-thousand letters, of which about three thousand have survived. In them we see supremely Vincent's talent as counsellor, director, and guide for troubled souls; his analysis touched by psychological finesse, and a deep wisdom that came from the Holy Spirit. He had such insight into human motivation; could see people's strengths

Chapel of Our Lady, Rue du Bac.

and weaknesses; and was adept at getting the best out of them.

Some needed to be encouraged, others to have the bar raised. If he had to admonish one of his community, he always admitted first that he himself had failed in many matters, but that with the grace of God they could both do better in the future. His advice was full of common sense and shrewdness.

Clearly he was astute in financial affairs, as he had to be, to manage all his complex and far-flung enterprises. Vincent, the realist, always stressed financial responsibility and prudence.

Helping the clergy

The fruit of the missions in the country parish would not endure unless the clergy were helped. So Vincent innovated short theology courses and spiritual preparation for those about to be ordained. Later, as seminaries became established, Vincent's priests would help to staff them. Next, there were workshops, in-service days and week-end retreats. Gradually the morale of the lower clergy was raised, and with it their pastoral effectiveness. And for many years Vincent served on a committee which advised on the appointment of bishops : thus the calibre of leadership in the Church steadily improved.

The spirit of Vincent in to-day's world

Fast-forward four centuries from Vincent's time, and the flame of his spirit still burns brightly. It lives on formally in more than two hundred communities, organisations and groups – not all of them Christian - that either have him as a patron, or look to him for inspiration.

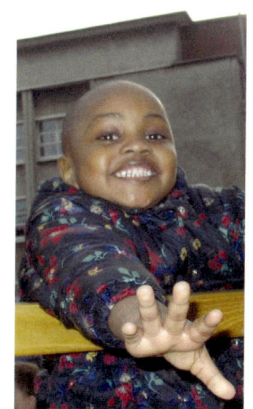

Frederic Ozanam.
Born 23 April 1813
Died 8 September 1853
Paris 1833. At the age of twenty, Frederic Ozanam founded the St Vincent de Paul Society. In 1997, Frederic Ozanam was beatified by Pope John Paul II.

The Sower: The seed is the Word of God.

His Vincentian priests still speak the saving Word of God on retreats and parish missions; still encourage and support their fellow-clergy; still pass on their educational expertise.

As for the Daughters - and there are about twenty-one thousand of them in ninety-three different countries – their hands-on, gentle charity still brings hope to the downcast. This shows itself in all sorts of ways: in arranging sheltered care for the elderly and accommodation for the homeless; in helping prisoners re-integrate; in caring for children and adults with intellectual disabilities; in hospice and home-care for the terminally ill; in recruiting and training foster parents; and in a thousand other interventions: their good works, seemingly without limit.

Of all the groups inspired by Vincent's charism, that have developed since his death, the best-known is surely the **Society of St. Vincent de Paul**, founded among a group of university students in Paris in 1833. Their leader was *Frederick Ozanam*.

The Society has local cells or "conferences" everywhere, composed of men and women, boys and girls, working quietly among the under-privileged in one hundred and thirty countries world-wide. They distribute food and clothing, run their own hostels, clubs and holiday homes; find employment; visit the sick and those in prison; smooth the path for migrants and refugees; grapple with the personal and social fall-out ensuing from addictions; as well as taking the initiative in countless other schemes and projects of justice and charity. Financial and skills assistance are provided for fellow-conferences in the third world. Their approach is low-key. They like to work unobtrusively. Their's, like Vincent's, is a practical charity that knows no distinction of class or creed or race; their values are the values of the Gospel of Jesus Christ.

Mission

Vincent's spirit was missionary, because it was the spirit of Jesus Christ: *"The Spirit of the Lord has anointed me, and sent me to speak Good News to the poor"* [Luke 4:18]. In his own lifetime, Priests and Daughters were sent out from France – even as far as Madagascar: a hazardous venture that suffered many losses. The first Vincentian martyr was slain cruelly in Limerick, Ireland, by Oliver Cromwell's forces. (He and Vincent were near-contemporaries).

And this missionary spirit continues for both his *Priests* and the *Daughters*, whether abroad in Kenya, Nigeria, Ethiopia, Fiji, the Cook Islands, and in other overseas countries; or here at home in Ireland and Britain. For it's of the essence of being a disciple of Jesus Christ to be on mission. That mission is everywhere, because the poor are everywhere. It's a mission for us in our homes, in our workplaces, in our neighbourhoods. Let the motto of the *Daughters*, taken from St. Paul, be our constant spur: *"the love of Christ keeps urging us onwards"* [2Cor 5:14].

Jim Mc Cormack C.M.

A blind Chinese priest and his server. Many Vincentian Priests and Daughters have missioned in China.

Some important dates

1581 Birth of Vincent de Paul in Pouy

1591 Birth of Louise de Marillac, near Paris

1600 Vincent ordained priest at Chateau l'éveque

1612 Appointed Parish Priest of Clichy-la-Garonne, near Paris; severe temptations against his Faith, which last three or four years

1613 Louise marries, and gives birth to a son : Michel Antoine.

1617 Vincent's mission sermon at Folleville; becomes Parish Priest of Chââtillon-les-Dombes (now, -sur-Chalaronne); first **Confraternity of Charity**, established in Chatillon.

1618 Vincent becomes friendly with Francis de Sales

1619 Appointed Chaplain to the Galleys

1622 Foundation of the **Congregation of the Mission** (Vincentians) Louise widowed.

1623 Vincent becomes Louise's Spiritual Director

1628 Takes possession of St.Lazare in Paris: motherhouse of the Vincentians

1633 The Bulla *Salvatoris Nostri* gives approval to the C.M. foundation of the **Daughters of Charity**

1634 Foundation of the **Ladies of Charity** of the Hôôtel Dieu

1638 Beginning of the work for foundlings.

1639 Beginning of relief - aid to war-ravaged Lorraine

1640 Vincent's mystical experience.

1641 Vincent's offer to resign as Superior of C.Ms not accepted by his confreres.

1642 Vincent joins the Council of Conscience for clergy appointments

1646 Vincentians sent to Algeria and Ireland

1647 Vincentians arrive in Madagascar. Letters of Vincent about frequent Holy Communion and against Jansenism

1651 Start of relief- aid to Picardy and Champagne. Mission to Limerick: death there of Vincentian proto-martyr Thaddeus Lee. Missionaries sent to Poland and to the Scottish Highlands and islands. Louise becomes a grand-mother.

1652 Vincent mediates in the second war of the Fronde and organises massive relief. D.Cs first foreign mission - to Warsaw.

1660 Death of Louise de Marillac (15th March), and of Vincent (27th September)

1729 Vincent declared Blessed by Pope Benedict X111, August 21st.

1737 Vincent declared a canonised Saint,16th June, by Pope Clement X11

1830 Apparitions of Our Lady to Sr. Catherine Labouré in the Rue du Bac.

1833 Foundation of the **St.Vincent de Paul Society** in Paris by Frederic Ozanam.

1934 Canonisation of Louise de Marillac, 11th March.

1997 Frederic Ozanam declared Blessed, August 22nd, in Notre Dame, Paris.